HIGH LEVEL SECURITY

Ben Hubbard

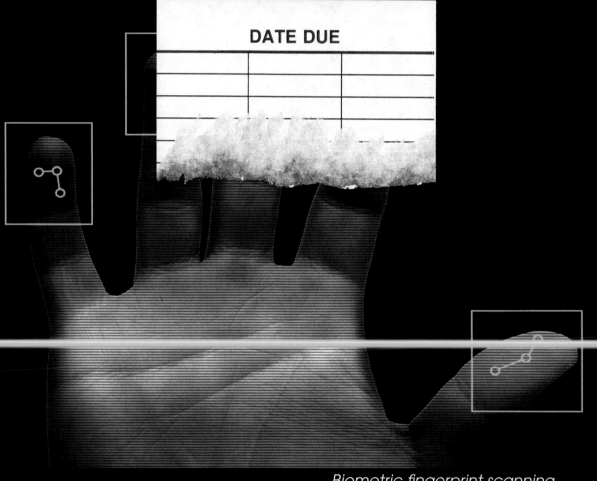

DATE DUE

Biometric fingerprint scanning

CLASH

by Tick Tock Books

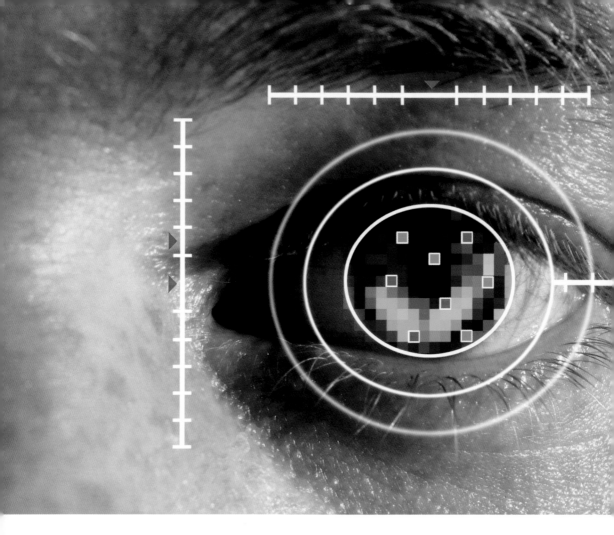

Publisher: Melissa Fairley
Art Director: Faith Booker
Editor: Victoria Garrard
Designer: Emma Randall
Production Controller: Ed Green
Production Manager: Suzy Kelly

ISBN: 978 1 84898 216 1

Picture credits (t=top; b=bottom; c=centre; l=left; r=right; OFC=outside front cover; OBC=outside):
AFP/Getty Images: 28–29. Andrew Brookes, National Physical Laboratory/Science Photo Library: 12b. Corbis/SuperStock:
15b. Courtesy of AeroVironment, Inc.: 21t. Courtesy of Emue Technologies: 23b. Ed Darack/Science Faction/Corbis: 9b.
Getty Images: 5b, 8, 16, 17t, 20–21. John Giles/PA Archive/Press Association Images: 19t. iStock: OFCl, OFC
(background), 5t, 6, OBCr, OBC (background). James King-Holmes/Science Photo Library: 10. Kim Kulish/Corbis: 17b.
Frans Lanting/Corbis: 13b. Pablo Paul/Alamy: 15t. Shutterstock: OFCtl, OFCbl, 1, 2, 4, 7t, 9t, 11, 12–13, 14, 18–19, 22,
23t, 24, 25, 26–27bc, OBCtr, OBCl. Time & Life Pictures/Getty Images: 26–27. www.janespencer.com: 7b.

Thank you to Lorraine Petersen and the members of nasen

Every effort has been made to trace copyright holders, and we apologize in advance for any omissions.
We would be pleased to insert the appropriate acknowledgements in any subsequent edition of this publication.

NOTE TO READERS
The website addresses are correct at the time of publishing. However, due to the ever-changing
nature of the Internet, websites and content may change. Some websites can contain links
that are unsuitable for children. The publisher is not responsible for changes in content or
website addresses. We advise that internet searches are supervised by an adult.

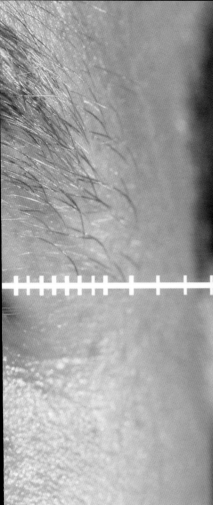

Iris recognition scan

CONTENTS

INTRODUCTION

Biometric eye scans

The modern world is all about technology. Technology makes our lives easier and safer. But how does it do this?

CCTV (closed-circuit television) monitors

Spy planes

The following pages explain the latest and greatest technology, from modern security in the home to biometrics and hi-tech spy planes.

HOME SECURITY

In medieval times, castles protected those inside with a moat, drawbridge and huge iron gates.

In the early 1900s, the first burglar alarms were installed in flats in New York City, USA.

Today, we rely on technology to keep our homes secure. Home security systems use keypad entry, motion sensors and CCTV cameras.

A keypad entry system

We can now control our security systems from a mobile phone, using a Web browser. This means we can watch what is going on inside our homes from anywhere in the world!

PANIC ROOMS

Homes owned by wealthy people sometimes contain secret panic rooms.

Often hidden in the basement, these rooms are built from reinforced concrete with a blast-proof steel door.

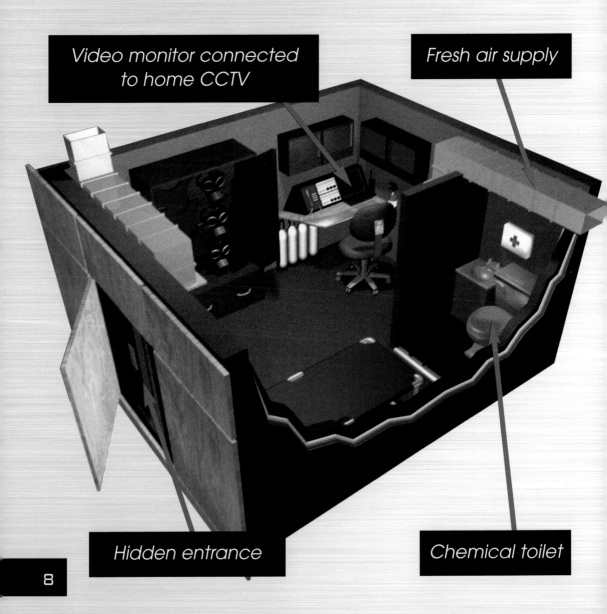

Video monitor connected to home CCTV

Fresh air supply

Hidden entrance

Chemical toilet

Simple panic rooms consist of a small room with a solid door and deadlock.

More expensive panic rooms use high-strength ballistic glass.

BIOMETRICS

Biometrics is like your own PIN (personal identification number) that nobody else can steal.

It works by recording a physical feature only you have, like your fingerprints. This information is stored on a database.

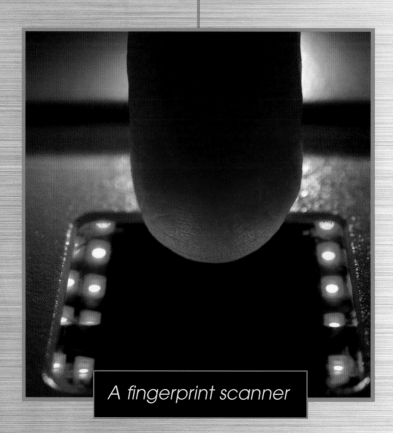

A fingerprint scanner

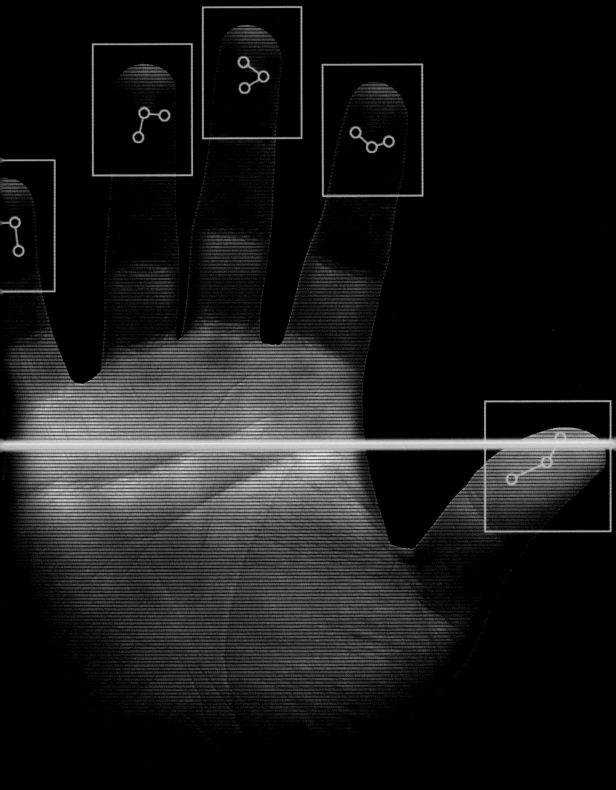

The shape and size of your hand can also be
biometrically scanned. The next time you place
your hand on the scanner, it recognizes you.

EYES AND VEINS

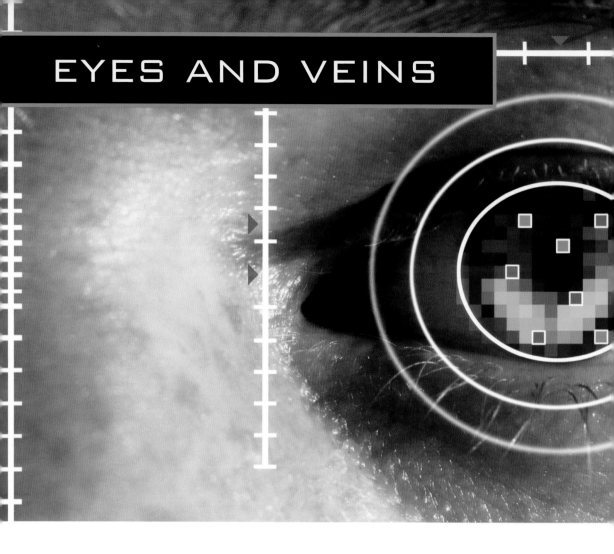

Iris recognition

A camera takes a photo of your iris – the coloured ring around the pupil in your eye. This is the safest biometric technology, because people's eyes do not change over time.

An iris recognition scanner

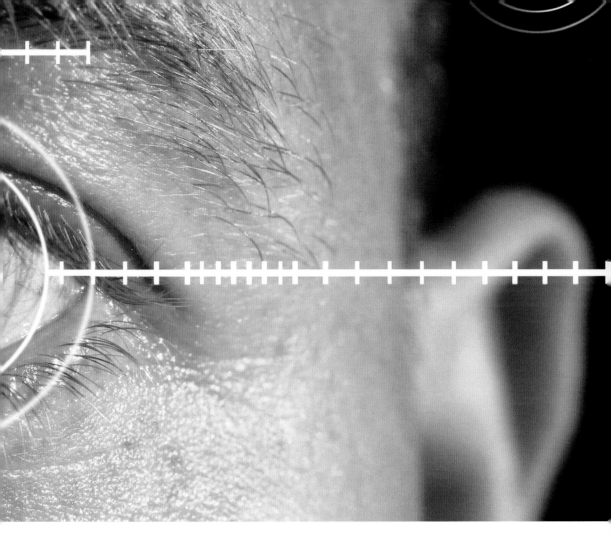

Vein scanning

A camera takes a picture of your wrist, finger or palm using infrared light. This light makes the blood in your veins appear black. The camera then records and stores the map of your veins.

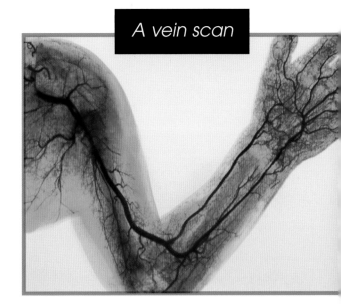

A vein scan

AIRPORTS

Every year, more than 1.5 billion people travel by aeroplane. Each of these passengers and their bags are checked for guns and explosives.

Luggage is searched at an airport.

Paperless tickets

Passengers download electronic tickets to their mobile phones, which are scanned at the airport.

Passports

Most passports now contain a biometric chip (see pages 10–11). Some airports also have biometric scanners for eyes and fingerprints.

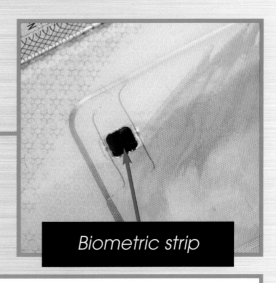

Biometric strip

Metal detectors

Every passenger has to pass through a metal detector. Hand-held metal detectors can locate exactly where a metal object is.

Hand-held metal detector

IMAGING AND ANALYSIS

X-ray machines
These machines scan your luggage and display the objects inside by shape and colour.

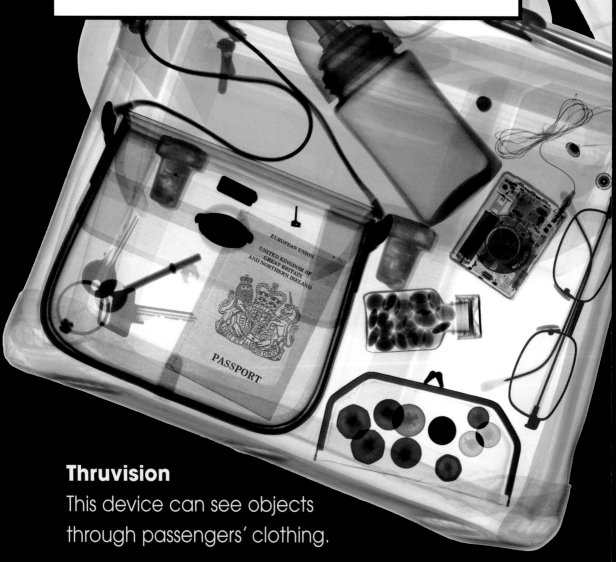

Thruvision
This device can see objects through passengers' clothing.

Imaging technology

This is like an X-ray for people, but instead of showing just a skeleton, it displays the passenger with his or her skin on!

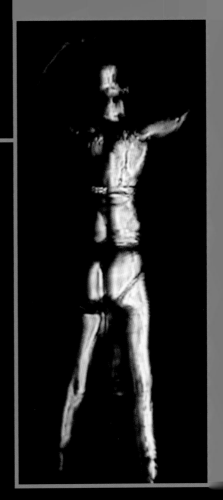

Explosives trace portals

These machines blow air onto passengers. They then analyze the air for traces of explosives.

SURVEILLANCE

CCTV cameras are everywhere. There are 4.2 million cameras in the UK alone! That's a fifth of all the CCTV cameras in the world.

The cameras send images to monitors, where police watch to see if someone is breaking the law.

Facial-recognition cameras can recognize and pick out a face from a crowd – perhaps a criminal on the run.

Police watch crowds with 'drones'. These are small remote-controlled helicopters, with a camera attached.

A police drone helicopter.

SPY PLANES

The United States Army uses remote-controlled spy planes to ensure certain areas are safe. They are called unmanned aerial vehicles (UAVs).

MQ-1 Predator

- Function: Surveillance and reconnaissance
- Wingspan: 14.8 metres
- Length: 8.22 metres
- Weight: 512 kilograms
- Speed: 217 kilometres per hour
- Range: Up to 730 kilometres
- Cameras: Three, including one infrared camera

Wasp III

- Function: Low-altitude surveillance
- Wingspan: 72.3 centimetres
- Length: 25.4 centimetres
- Weight: 430 grams
- Speed: Between 32 and 64 kilometres per hour
- Cameras: Two day/night cameras

CREDIT CARDS

Credit card theft is a big problem.

People often steal credit cards or copy the cards' details. They can then use the cards to buy items online, over the phone or by post. They do not need a card's PIN to do this.

However a new card hopes to end this. The Emue card has its own display screen and keypad.

When you type your PIN into the card, it displays a new number. Without this number, the card is useless. It comes up with a different number every time, so only the PIN holder can use it.

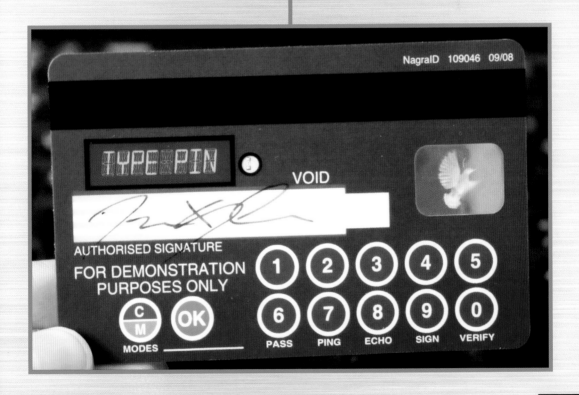

NagraID 109046 09/08

TYPE*PIN

VOID

AUTHORISED SIGNATURE

FOR DEMONSTRATION
PURPOSES ONLY

MODES

C
M

OK

1 2 3 4 5
6 7 8 9 0

PASS PING ECHO SIGN VERIFY

BODYGUARDS

Close protection officers (CPOs) are specially trained to physically protect people from harm.

World leaders often have a small army of CPOs to protect them against assassins – people hired to kill them.

CPO skills
- A background in the police force or army
- Expert at martial arts
- Trained in guns and weapons
- Observant and quick-thinking
- Calm under pressure

CPO gadgets

- A non-lethal weapon
- Baton, pepper spray, Taser™ or electric stun gun
- Defensive flashlight
- Fully automatic machine pistol
- Kevlar bullet proof vest
- Covert earpiece and radio set
- Tuffwriter defensive pen – writes under the most extreme conditions
- Handcuffs

FORT KNOX

Fort Knox, in Kentucky, USA, is the most secure building in the world. It is a fortress protected by a state-of-the-art security system and armed guards.

Underneath is a vault containing billions of dollars in US government gold bars.

The vault is lined with granite walls and
a door weighing more than 20 tonnes.

No visitors are allowed
inside the vault.

THE BEAST

12-centimetre-thick blast-proof glass windows.

Kevlar-reinforced tyres with steel wheels.

The US President's limousine is called "The Beast". It is the most advanced and secure protection vehicle in the world.

12-centimetre-thick armour plating

Weighs about six tonnes

Armoured fuel tank

Only a few Secret Service agents know what it is capable of, and they are sworn to secrecy!

assassin Someone who murders someone else, usually a leader, for political or religious reasons.

biometrics The process of measuring and storing information about the human body.

closed-circuit television (CCTV) A system in which one or more cameras transmit moving images to monitors.

drawbridge A bridge that can be raised and lowered.

infrared A short wavelength of invisible radiation that can detect heat.

Kevlar A special man-made fibre of great strength.

moat A deep ditch surrounding a castle, usually filled with water.

monitor A computer screen.

motion sensor A device that triggers an alarm or light by detecting movement.

reconnaissance A military operation carried out to observe an area of land in order to locate an enemy.

Secret Service The US agency that protects current and former presidents.

surveillance Close observation of a person or people.

DID YOU KNOW?

- The UK has one per cent of the world's population but 20 per cent of the world's CCTV cameras.

- Biometric security is used at Disneyland – fingerprint scanners are used at the funpark to stop people sharing their admission tickets.

SECURITY ONLINE

Dedicated to homeland security in the USA, targeted for kids:
www.fema.gov/kids/nse

Website about security at airports:
www.howstuffworks.com/airport-security.htm

Website for MI5, the agency that protects the UK against threats to national security:
www.mi5.gov.uk

National Security Agency (NSA) website, with information about keeping the USA safe:
www.nsa.gov

The United States Secret Service website:
www.secretservice.gov

INDEX